In Their Own Words

Recollections of an Earlier Loudoun

Photographs by Sarah Huntington
Interviews by Gale Waldron
Foreword by Henry Taylor

Cover and text design by Lisa Hawthorne
Book production by Claire Coughter

The publisher would like to thank Janet Matthews for supplying the photograph
of Vinton Pickens by Andres Alonso on page 61, and William Marable
for conducting the initial interviews that are contained on pages 13, 35, and 41.
Frontispiece photo of Esther Cowart and Dr. Joe Rogers.

ISBN: Softcover   978-1-4771-3724-6
        Hardcover 978-1-4771-3725-3
        Ebook   978-1-4771-3726-0

Print information available on the last page.

Rev. date: 04/27/2019

To order additional copies of this book, contact:
Xlibris
1-888-795-4274
www.Xlibris.com
Orders@Xlibris.com

Dedication

To the storytellers in this book

Foreword by Henry Taylor

Introduction

Portraits

Acknowledgments

Contents

I write this a week after the death of Asa Moore Janney, a powerful presence in my life from the moment I was able to recognize people. He had an unusually keen sense of the passage of time and the effects of progress, for he had seen more than one way of life dwindle down to history as another took its place. The glass case beside his desk in the Lincoln store held documents and artifacts that he could identify and explain, and he would do that for anyone who expressed interest, because he believed that these things could tell us where we had come from. I believe he was right about that.

The monologues and images gathered here, various in tone, remind me that the line is thin and wavering between celebration and elegy. Some of them are humorous, a few are sad or even angry, but all of them recall with deep affection a time and place that fewer and fewer of us actually remember. I know how it feels to poke around in a barn I haven't seen in years, and to turn up there a tool or a piece of harness or other equipment that I used to handle regularly. There is a peculiar blend of feelings: sorrow that its useful days are gone, elation that I know what it is and can remember how those days were.

So, though I miss the countryside from which these voices and pictures rose, I am grateful to have this beautiful reminder of how it was to live in it.

—Henry Taylor

Foreword

Henry Taylor was born and raised in Lincoln where his family has farmed land since the early 1700s. A professor of literature and the Co-Director of the MFA program in Creative Writing at The American University in Washington, DC, he is the author of five collections of poetry, including The Flying Change for which he received the Pulitzer Prize in 1986.

Fifty five miles from the nation's capitol and once connected to it by railroad tracks, Loudoun County used to be a farming community where agriculture supplied jobs, food, and even entertainment. Those tracks and much of the farmland that depended on them are covered over now, the way having been paved for a newer Loudoun, one that is touted as the second fastest growing county in the country. Change is now constant here, and what was once called country living is all but a distant memory.

Memories live on, however, so we thought it might be a good idea to collect some of them. About four years ago we set out to talk to some of Loudoun's older folks who could tell us about earlier times. From Ashburn to Bluemont, we met with farmers, store owners, horse trainers, newsmen, railroad workers, politicians, bankers, doctors, and men of the church. We talked to them about their memories, we took their photographs, and we documented their stories.

As the interviews took place, we discovered more than we dreamed we would. We heard about old villages, lost roads, fall harvests, hog butcherings, bootlegged whiskey, card games, and tent revivals. We learned about the restoration of Waterford, Middleburg's hunt country, WPA projects in Lovettsville, and the first court-ordered subdivision in Sterling. And we had the honor to meet some of the men and women who remember Loudoun long before all of the changes brought by growth.

This book is both a collection of their personal experiences and a tribute to that earlier Loudoun. Each story stands on its own. Together, they create a sort of history of a special place in a different time—a time of family farms, small towns, and neighborhood villages—a time when people felt a sense of place and community. A time well worth remembering.

Listen to them now as they share their memories—in their own words.

Introduction

It was early in the morning, a Monday in March, 1926. A burglar started the fire—he dropped a match, I guess. He was trying to steal clothing from the apparel shop evidently, because fancy clothes were strewn all over the store.

The stores were very close together—there was a hardware store, a post office, and a meat shop too. The Hamilton Mercantile and its shoe store were there, and the drug store, and a men's haberdashery. The fire started at the apparel shop, and it went on for three days.

We ran out of water here; all the wells were pumped dry. Fire companies came from all over—Leesburg, Winchester, Manassas, Frederick—even from Washington. Everybody brought buckets of water and lined up to fight the fire.

I can remember how hot it was. They tried to keep the fire from spreading across the street and destroying the houses there, so they watered everything down heavily. That line of evergreen trees stopped the fire from spreading across the street. But all the stores burned to the ground, and all the businesses were displaced.

No one was hurt, but it was a devastation of Hamilton. We never found that burglar either.

Esther Cowart

Born and raised in Hamilton, Esther Cowart now lives around the corner from the site of the big fire. For years, she worked for her father, Howard Rogers, a former member of the Board of Supervisors and a state legislator. Later, she helped out at Jane's Kindergarten, her sister's private school in Hamilton. A former trustee of Loudoun Memorial Hospital, Esther has served on the Ladies Board since 1939. She is a charter member of the Loudoun Preservation Society and a former trustee of the Hamilton Baptist Church.

I spent my earliest years in Morrisonville when there was no electricity, gas, plumbing, or central heating. The workday ended when it got dark, and after dinner we'd all sit out on the porch and talk about the wisdom of the ages. I remember my grandmother in her rocker and my Uncle Irvey presiding over the group and uttering the words he would utter time and time again: "A man works from sun to sun, but a woman's work is never done."

No greater truth was ever spoken! Those women were up at dawn and they'd work all day long. It was backbreaking work.

Cooking was a tremendous job because the women cooked on wood-fired, cast iron stoves. There was no turning on the stove to 350 degrees. They had to get the kindling, they had to start the fire, they had to get it up to the proper heat. In the morning, they did housecleaning, and that was just the beginning. The garden had to be tended to because they grew their own food. Most places had a hog or two, and there were chickens, of course, and eggs to get.

Every day of the week had a job attached to it. Monday was laundry and that meant hauling water from the spring, boiling it, and scrubbing clothes. Tuesday was ironing and that meant heating those heavy pieces of metal on the woodstove to get them hot. And there was a day for patching because all of our clothes had to be maintained. Slop jars had to be emptied out, cleaned, and fumigated. It was endless labor.

The period of time I'm talking about is the late '20s and early '30s. This is the age of Scott Fitzgerald who is having the time of his life in New York, and in Morrisonville it was as though the 20th century hadn't yet arrived.

Russell Baker

Russell Baker's career in journalism included reporting for the Baltimore Sun and writing a column for the New York Times. The author of several books, he received the Pulitzer Prize for biography for Growing Up, which was published in 1982. Now retired, he lives in Leesburg.

When I moved to Loudoun in 1931 there were only 1,500 people living in Leesburg. Years later, in 1949, I ran for Town Council, and there were fourteen people in that race. I knew I wouldn't be elected, but I ran for a reason. You see, on my way to work one morning I overheard two black men complaining about some of the problems Leesburg was having at the time. So I asked those guys, why didn't they run for office and make an effort to improve things. They told me that black people couldn't be included in the town election.

So we made a little bet right there that I would run. We were big time spenders—bet 50 cents apiece. You laugh, but that was a considerable amount back then. Anyhow, I was determined to prove to them that I could do it. So during my lunch break, I went on over to the Courthouse and registered and filed my papers to be in the race for Town Council.

Well, when the votes were counted, I had come in seventh.

I didn't win that election, but I did win the money from those two guys.

John Tolbert

The first black man to run for public office in Loudoun County, John Tolbert later served on the Leesburg Town Council for 14 years, from 1976 to 1990, and never missed a meeting. Active in public life, he gave his time and energy to numerous organizations and committees, receiving a number of awards for his achievements. Tolbert Street and the Tolbert building, both in Leesburg, are named in his honor. He died in 1999.

Reproduction courtesy of Loudoun Art, Amendment I Inc.

We were both city folk—my husband was from Baltimore, and I was from New York and Chicago. I wanted to be a writer or an actress, and he was interested in farming. So we bought Temple Hall Farm in 1940, and I lived there for the next 47 years.

Neither of us knew the first thing about farming, but we were eager to learn and took to it right away—the animals, the land, and the changing seasons. We started raising popcorn, which was very, very successful. That was when the popcorn market was at its peak. Popcorn was similar to field corn—it had a small stalk and small ear, and really, if you saw a field of it, you wouldn't know it was popcorn.

Before we harvested the popcorn, we'd take off some of the grains to see if they were dried out enough. We'd pick it in the daytime, starting in the early morning, and then we'd pack it into 100-pound bags and drive it in the truck at night to Winchester and Washington so it would be ready for the early morning markets.

But the popcorn market plummeted in 1944 and so we had to do something else. We went into cattle and hogs then, which was what everybody else was doing at the time, and we learned how to take care of them and the chickens, ducks, and horses too.

The Northern Virginia Parks Authority acquired Temple Hall in 1985. I spent years looking for the right organization to take over the care of the property, and they told me they would tend to the land and keep it as an educational facility and a working farm. They don't do things the way I would, of course, but the farm is still there, and no developer can get his hands on my beloved land.

Mrs. J.H. Symington

Mrs. Symington lived and worked on Temple Hall Farm's 286 acres for 47 years before the Parks Authority acquired the property. She lives in Leesburg now, and is the only woman member of the Catoctin Farmer's Club, the oldest in the county.

It was probably 1935 or '36, and there was a bit of stealing going on in those days. So, many was the time I stayed in the store at night with my shotgun. You never heard the store creak so. The wind would blow and—creak—you'd look at that window, and then—creak—you'd look at the door. It kept me pretty busy, I tell you.

One night, I asked Bert French to watch the store for me. It was probably about 1:00 a.m. when Bert opened the door to let the cat in and started to step back inside. All of a sudden, here comes this guy, BAM, puts down his gas can, then BAM, puts down another gas can, and comes right up on the porch and opens up the screen door that fast. Bert said the guy wasn't even trying to sneak around; he acted like he owned the place. He had taken the tumblers out of the door lock the night before, see, so that any key could open the door, and tonight he was going to steal some gasoline.

Well, Bert didn't know what to do, but he was pretty nervous. What got into him, I don't know, but in all the excitement he broke the cat's tail and then he threw that cat right in the face of the intruder. That poor guy, he stumbled backwards and fell right off the porch. I got there a bit later and saw those two gasoline cans and the man's hat lying there, and I knew something had happened. And there was Bert petting the cat, and the cat's tail was all bent out of shape.

Asa Moore Janney

Born in 1908, Asa Moore Janney was the postmaster of the Lincoln Post Office from 1932 to 1972. He was also a farmer and a builder of houses and barns. Renowned for his stories, Asa Moore wrote several books about Loudoun country life, and they are available at the Janney Store in Lincoln, the site of this true story. Asa Moore died in 2002. Reproduction courtesy of Loudoun Art, Amendment 1 Inc.

I came to Waterford in 1938 when I married Wellman Chamberlin. Wellman had grown up at Clifton, the Chamberlin family farm just outside of town. His two brothers, Edward and LeRoy, started the restoration of Waterford in the 1920s. That was during the depression of course. The town was pretty run down then, and the brothers were able to give people work.

LeRoy and Edward restored the Arch House for us newlyweds to live in. I'll never forget Uncle Edward walking across the scaffolding. He was blind you know, and I could never understand how he could do that. But he was the one who had the interest in architecture and restoration, while LeRoy had the eyes, the desire, and the wherewithal to get things done. They restored a number of houses in the middle of town along Main and Second Streets, and the Quaker Meeting House too.

Their work started something in Waterford. Other people began to fix up their houses and eventually the town was almost completely done over. It looks today almost like it did 200 years ago, although it was never quite as spiffy as it is now.

I remember being surrounded for miles by farmland and my boys working with the farmers in the summers, riding combines and making hay. They played all over the countryside and swam in the Catoctin creek, and we never worried much about the dangers they might run into. Life was slower and more relaxed then.

Waterford was such a nice small country town and a good place to raise a family. My mother said to me many times over the years, "Now don't let yourself go just because you're living in the country," but I thoroughly enjoyed it. I just loved being there.

Anne Carter Smith

Anne Carter Smith came to Waterford as a young bride and raised her family there. Always active in her community, she was a member of the Waterford Players and the Waterford Choral Group. She lived in Waterford from 1938 until 2001. She now lives in Leesburg.

I'll never forget the night I won the most money ever in a poker game. There was a junkman convention over in Frederick at one of the hotels. Well, junkmen deal in cash, and after the meeting there was a big poker game. Seemed like the cards was coming my way, and the rest of the boys was drinking liquor so the bets were getting bigger and bigger. There it was—I was six thousand dollars ahead and knew it was time to go. Well, you can't get up and leave a game if you're winning like that, so I excused myself between deals, went over to the bar, and bought a fifth of whiskey. I set that bottle of whiskey on the table and said, "Good evening, gentlemen, I've got to go."

It was just past midnight when I walked out of there and started driving back home down Old 180; that was before the new road to Frederick. I hadn't gotten far out of town when a car came up behind me. Back then there wasn't any traffic and the area wasn't all grown up in houses. Well, I gave them the wave to pass several times, but they just kept on my tail and I started getting nervous, you know, with that roll of money on me.

After about ten miles, I thought, well, let's just get this over with. So I pulled into the lot of the old church outside Jefferson, thinking here it comes. Well, that car went on by and I said out loud, "Thank the Lord." I drove on home and the next day bought my wife a brand new automobile.

Kingfish Everhart

Kingfish Everhart claims he made a living in Loudoun doing a little bit of everything, including working on the railroad and digging graves. A licensed junk dealer from 1939 to his retirement in 1975, he bought and sold whatever he could, including a DC7 airplane and over 10,000 cars. He won't say how he got his nickname.
Reproduction courtesy of Loudoun Art, Amendment I Inc.

In my day, postmasters were political jobs. In the town of Hillsboro, Mr. and Mrs. Mann alternated the position, depending on who was President. She was a Democrat, you see, and he was a Republican.

So, first off, you had to have your politics right, and it happened that there was a Democratic president and a Republican senate. The postmaster in those days had to be recommended by his U.S. senator, appointed by his president, and confirmed by the senate. So in that order, I was recommended by Harry Byrd, appointed by Harry Truman, and confirmed by the Republican senate. I took office January 1st, 1948, but I didn't get the postmaster job until June 16th.

The delay was that the Republican senate held up my appointment because I was a Democrat.

But it went through eventually because Franklin Roosevelt had outsmarted the Republicans. Being a wartime president, he was able to slip a few things through congress here and there, and he had taken all of the postmasters out of the political arena and put them in civil service. So in order to be a postmaster you had to have a good score on the civil service examination. Well, of the seventeen people who applied for the job, I had the top score.

And I fell in love with the job even if it didn't pay any money. Heck, the Safeway store manager in Purcellville made ten times as much as the postmaster did in those days—well maybe not ten times but a lot more. But I enjoyed the people I worked with, and I liked what we were doing for people. I was with the Purcellville Post Office for 25 years, and I just had a good time with it.

Hugh Grubb

*Postmaster by day, Hugh Grubb was also a professional photographer
who worked many evenings in his darkroom. He and his wife, Mary Esther,
live on the family's 250-acre farm near Hillsboro.*

Nowadays, you can't tell what season it is by the clothes the kids are wearing. In my day, the clothes were thin in the summer and thick in the winter. We hurried Spring as fast as we could so that we could take off our shoes and go barefoot, which we did all summer long. And we swam in the creek. We weren't required to bathe every night, but we did have to wash our feet every night.

People always ask me what I did for entertainment when I was growing up. Well, everything I did was entertainment. Even the winters were fun for kids. One of the things I did in the wintertime was to trap animals, something that's frowned on today. It's illegal, I think. But back then, I caught skunks, and I skinned them. I saved the odor of the skunk and put it in a vial so that I would have it for special occasions.

I'd often use the scent on hog butchering day. That was an exciting day for me, and I always wanted to stay home from school to be a part of it. But my parents thought it was more important for me to go to school to get an education. So here's what I would do: I'd put that skunk oil on my shoes, and then I'd go off to school and sit near the stove. It wouldn't be too long before they'd send me home.

My father never said anything about it, but I'm pretty sure he put two and two together.

Tom Taylor

Tom Taylor was born in 1911 and was raised in a Lincoln farmhouse built in 1827 by his great grandfather. Originally a dairy farm, the Taylor land is now operated for cattle and corn. A farmer and foxhunter, Tom also taught English at Loudoun Valley High School in the 1960s. He died in 2001. Reproduction courtesy of Loudoun Art, Amendment I Inc.

My daddy was a farmer, and I grew up on the Clifford Farm just west of Oatlands. Major Clifford, that's what we called him, let me ride his horses. I used to ride from the farm to the Oatland's store which was two or three miles away, right along the Goose Creek. And the faster I rode, the better I liked it.

Mrs. Russell ran the store, and I'd go there to buy candy or bread or something. There was a post office in the village then, and a blacksmith shop, an old mill, and quite a few houses.

But the transportation department came along and redid the road. That was in the 1940s, and the new road divided the village in half. Today you'd never know it was there at all. You can still see parts of the old road, but they did away with the store, the post office, and the old steel bridge that went across the creek too. I liked that old bridge.

I went to Mountain Gap School which is where I met Bill, my husband. It was a one-room schoolhouse for seven grades, and Miss Goss was our teacher. I remember she'd let the boys play on the mountain behind the school, but the girls weren't allowed. And when one of the boys was bad, the others would go out in the woods and bring back a switch for the teacher to whip him with. If the girls were naughty, they'd have to stand on one foot in the corner for ten minutes. But they didn't get a whipping.

And I remember Miss Goss sending us down to the spring with a bucket to fetch water, and we'd all drink out of the same dipper. No one ever got sick from it either.

Helen Harris Moss

Helen Harris Moss was born in 1914 and has lived in Loudoun all of her life. She resides in the 200-year-old house where her husband, William, was born. William Moss worked at Oatlands in the gardens and the greenhouse. Built in 1884, Mountain Gap School is a property of the National Trust for Historic Preservation and a Virginia Historic Landmark.

There's a sign at the barber shop: "You can't get rich in a small town. Too many people are watching."

Well, when I was growing up in Leesburg, it was a small town and a good place to grow up. In 1950, when I was 12, the town had 1,800 people, I think, and the county had about 20,000 people. It was a community: everybody knew everybody, and we all looked out for one another. Leesburg had a lot of neighborhoods then—Vinegar Hill, Georgetown, Murderer's Bay—and at the town limits, the farms started abruptly and there were open fields as far as you could see.

And everybody had a role. We had the town drunks, one for each social class, the town bootlegger, the town homosexual, and even the village idiot. The town had one policeman and the sheriff's department had only four or five deputies. There weren't many people then who commuted to work. Everything we needed was in town.

The community wasn't segregated, as many communities were at the time in the south. The schools were, but after school we all played ball together. There were no organized amusements, either. The kids made their own activities. We could go anywhere and do anything without worrying about any harm coming to us, the way people have to worry now.

I remember one time I was at home and saw smoke coming from the basement. My mother was gone, so I picked up the phone, and when Nellie the operator said, "Number, please," I asked her to help find my mother. Well, it was a small town, and Nellie happened to know that my mother was playing bridge over at Mrs. Clemens' house. So she called over there and mother came home right away to check on things. There wasn't any fire though, so she went back to her bridge game.

Reverend Elijah B. White, III

Reverend White has been the Rector of the Church of Our Saviour near Oatlands for the past 25 years. He was Editor of the Loudoun Times-Mirror in the 1960s before entering seminary. A missionary in the Fiji Islands for several years, Reverend White returned to Loudoun in 1977 to serve the parish he had helped as a seminarian.

My dad came to Loudoun in 1923 and was the vet for Morven Park. I guess I followed in his footsteps.

I've doctored just about every kind of animal there is, from a rattlesnake to an elephant. But I'd have to say I enjoyed the horses most of all. The small animals get too complicated, and their owners always seemed to me to be far more unreasonable.

When I started my practice in 1945 we were on call 24 hours a day, and I was called to the scene of a lot of animal emergencies. Once I had to get under an overturned horse trailer over there by Clark's Gap. I had to crawl in between the horse's legs to tranquilize him so we could slide him out from under there.

I remember one year at the hunt club ball when I got an emergency call for a horse with colic. It wasn't my client, and I was in my tuxedo, but I went over there to treat the horse. Well, it turns out that horse's vet was at the same party, but he was having a good time dancing and didn't want to take the call. Those people didn't change vets either.

Sure, I had a few close calls. A farm in Upperville had a short-horned bull with a sore foot that needed treating. That bull weighed about two tons, but it stood there real nice for me, and so I went to put a heavy-duty halter over his horns. But when I cinched the halter and started to pull on it, that rascal lunged and caught me between his horns and the wall. Somehow I shimmied up the wall and over to the other stall and got away. Two days later, that same bull gored his owner to death.

Dr. Jack Howard

One of a few large animal practitioners, Dr. Howard established Leesburg's first veterinary hospital in 1954. He practiced veterinary medicine for over 50 years, retiring in 1995. In that time, he trained many of Loudoun's veterinarians, including Doctors Rokus, Horne, Pease, and Diehl.

I lived in St. Louis in the '60s, and I got involved in the civil rights movement and the NAACP. Then, when I moved to Purcellville, I worked with the War on Poverty. I went to a lot of meetings for these causes because I wanted to do my part to make it happen the way I believed was the right way. And I started going regularly to the County Board of Supervisors meetings too. It was a learning process for me and a real eye-opener. There weren't that many black people who went to the Supervisor meetings because it was almost an unwritten law that black people weren't supposed to. But I felt I had a right to be there.

My favorite subject to talk to them about was education, because education is what we all need to live a better life. I think I was considered some kind of oddity, but I always tried to make a point. Many times I would quote something from Abraham Lincoln or Thomas Jefferson, because I figured their words carried more weight than anything I could say. Other times, I would try to point out to them that even though they had done their homework, they might have missed an important fact or two. I think I brought to the Board members a different kind of lifestyle perspective, not a landowner's or a businessman's.

After a while, I think they kind of looked forward to me coming to their meetings and wondered what I was going to say next. I'm sure they thought, "that woman is either very brave or she's crazy as heck."

Lou Etta Watkins

Lou Etta Watkins was raised in Rectortown. In 1952, she moved to St. Louis just outside Middleburg, and later to Leesburg, where she's lived with her husband, Frank, for the last 33 years. She is an active volunteer with the League of Women Voters, the Library Foundation, the Alliance for the Mentally Ill, the Democratic Party, and the NAACP.

I was just a farmer in Bluemont milking cows, and politics was the furthest thing from my mind.

In those days, getting the Democratic nomination meant getting elected. Even so, there was always a token Republican. But in 1967, there were three Democrats on the ballot, and the two conservative Democrats split the vote so that the third candidate, a liberal, snuck through.

Well, I became the Republican candidate, and it was the classic political phenomenon. They didn't vote for me; they voted against her. And that's how I got in.

We used to meet in the old hotel building in town. When I got on the board, I was more anti-growth than people are now. I represented the farmer and I was pro-environment. I was the only Republican on the Board for years.

The first thing we tried to do was get a bottle bill in the county, and we ended up passing one but the state threw it out. We were becoming progressive, getting new ideas about planning and zoning. Sterling Park had come in, and nobody knew what the implications would be, but we were beginning to understand the need for building and plumbing codes and that kind of thing to protect the home buyer.

At the height of our anti-growth efforts, a big developer came in to talk about building Countryside, and we turned him down because we wanted to stop and take a hard look at things. Those developers took us to court, and Countryside became the first court-ordered development.

It's ironic. I got on the board representing the farmers. Back then, the farmers were opposed to Sterling Park because of what the development would do to the tax base. Nowadays, most farmers support growth because it keeps the value of their land.

Jim Brownell

Jim Brownell first moved to Loudoun in 1946, and then again in 1959 when he took over the dairy operations at White Hall Farm in Bluemont where he raised his family. He served on the Board of Supervisors for 24 years, retiring in 1991.

The very first job I had was Editor of the Loudoun News. Mr. Hall owned the paper then, and he offered me the job. I worked for him for three or four years in the early '40s. The paper had a paid circulation of about 700 and a total circulation of about 1,500.

The Loudoun News was a weekly paper. On Monday and Tuesday, we would go get the news. Then, on Wednesday, I would check the proof. On Thursday the paper would come out, and I'd have to take copies to Lovettsville because if you sent them by train they wouldn't get there for four days. On Friday, Saturday, and Sunday, we'd go out and sell as many ads as we could. It was a 75- to 80-hour work week, and I was paid $20 a week.

I did everything except run the Linotype machine. Thomas did that, and he had to get two galleys an hour from the Linotype in order for us to get the paper out on time. Well, when we started getting only one galley an hour and a whole lot of mistakes, we'd know that Thomas was back there drinking. I remember one time I went back there to see what was going on and there sat Thomas, not doing anything.

So I went over to him and put my hand on his shoulder, and he fell right over. I took him home to his wife and told her I needed her help: "We've got to sober him up fast, because it's Wednesday and we've got to get the paper out."

Frank Raflo

Frank Raflo was born in Leesburg in 1919 and was the Editor of the Loudoun News from 1942–1949. He served one term as mayor of the town of Leesburg (1961 to 1963) and also served on the Board of Supervisors from 1972 to 1986. Known for his colorful storytelling, he is the author of two books: Within the Iron Gates and Hauntings and Happenings.
Reproduction courtesy of Loudoun Art, Amendment I Inc.

As a child I spent every summer in Lovettsville. My sister and I were from Washington and as soon as school let out, we'd come here, and we just loved it. My mother's best friend was Cecilia McKimmey George, and she took us in for the entire summer.

It was the 1920s and the George's—I called them Aunt Cecilia and Uncle Henry—had two farms which adjoined each other. Of course, Loudoun had some of the most fertile fields of any place in the world. The farmers had a sort of co-op then and they moved from one farm to another to bring in the wheat or hay, and they used horses to do it. And while they worked on each farm, the women would cook the meals. You see, each farm wife would try to outdo the other one with the dinner. They wanted to hear the men say, "Oh, that's the finest meal I ever had." And what meals they were!

We'd hear the jingle of the horses coming across the fields, and we'd cry out, "Here come the men." And there was such a flurry of activity to get everything to the kitchen table. All these huge dishes of vegetables and meats, big platters of corn on the cob, all kinds of fruits, pies, cakes, and preserves, and milk to drink. We even had honeycombs.

And when the men finished eating, they were so stuffed they could hardly move. They'd get up, push their chairs back, and go outside. And it would be hotter than the dickens, and they'd lie in the shade and take a nap. And they needed it. That's the truth!

Billie Hetzel

Billie Hetzel continues to be passionate about homegrown produce. She moved to Loudoun permanently in 1962 with her husband, Fred, and grew organic vegetables, selling them on Saturdays at the Leesburg Farmer's Market at various locations over the years. To attract attention to her farm stand, she dressed up in old-fashioned clothes and sunbonnets. Today, she grows organic vegetables on her family farm outside Purcellville. Reproduction courtesy of Loudoun Magazine, Amendment I Inc.

I was born right down the road where the townhouses are now. We moved to this farm when I was nine months old—that was March of 1909.

My parents were in the dairy business when I was coming up. So when I was a young boy, I don't remember exactly how old I was, I said I wanted to get up really early and learn about milking the cows. Well, I was stuck from then on getting the milk to the train. We'd have to get up at 4:00 a.m., milk the cows, cool the milk, put it into cans, and take it to Purcellville by 6:03—that's when the milk train came to take the milk into Washington.

I did that until I was 13 years old, until 1922. My father died that year and my mother couldn't handle the dairy farm herself; the men who had worked for my father wouldn't take orders from a woman. So she worked into the chicken business. We raised baby chickens, and we had a custom hatchery. People would bring in eggs that they wanted hatched, and we'd charge a fee to hatch them in our incubator.

We gradually worked into selling chickens, and the business grew. At that period, all those chicken farms over on the Eastern Shore were just getting started. But there weren't many chicken farms around here then, and people would come from all over the area on Fridays and Saturdays and we'd sell them live chickens for their Sunday dinners.

We had a few thousand chickens then, and we did pretty good. We had to be there all the time, but it wasn't heavy labor. And I didn't have to get up at 4:00 in the morning.

Howell Brown

Howell Brown lives on Crooked Run Farm in Purcellville, his family farm for six generations. His son, Sam, operates the farm now for pick-your-own fruit, vegetables, and flowers. Crooked Run Farm is just east of Purcellville.

"LawNee," that's how my mother used to call me. "LawNee." You could hear her for a mile. I grew up wild as a buck in them North Carolina mountains. Bought my first Ford car in 1936—a coup. A lot of people said that Brown boy would never amount to anything. I made, sold, and drank that mountain water, you know. The old devil had me good then.

Then one night I went to a tent revival, and the preacher there got a hold of me. "God can change your life if you ask him. Test me," he said, "test me."

That started it right there. I sat alone in the dark woods and opened up the Holy Book. Lightning bugs came and lit on the pages as I read the words that saved me from darkness. I've been preaching ever since. I pastored that church in Paeonian Springs, and I built my own church in Hamilton—every last board of it—with my own hands.

They ran me off for my preaching. I've been threatened with arrest for preaching on the street about working on Sunday. I've preached to the congregation, and they all started to sing, drowning me out. But the Lord has kept me. Many's the time the doctor told me I'd never get out of bed, never drive another nail. But I know that doctor ain't God. Only God knows I'm here, still preaching, still going on.

See all these Bibles? I wore them out, and more besides.

Reverend Lawnie J. Brown

The Reverend Lawnie Brown moved to Paeonian Springs and pastored the Pentecostal Church there from 1947–1953. He built his own church in Hamilton in 1953. Although he lost much of his voice in 1955, he continued to preach at revivals and other meeting places. He died in 2001.

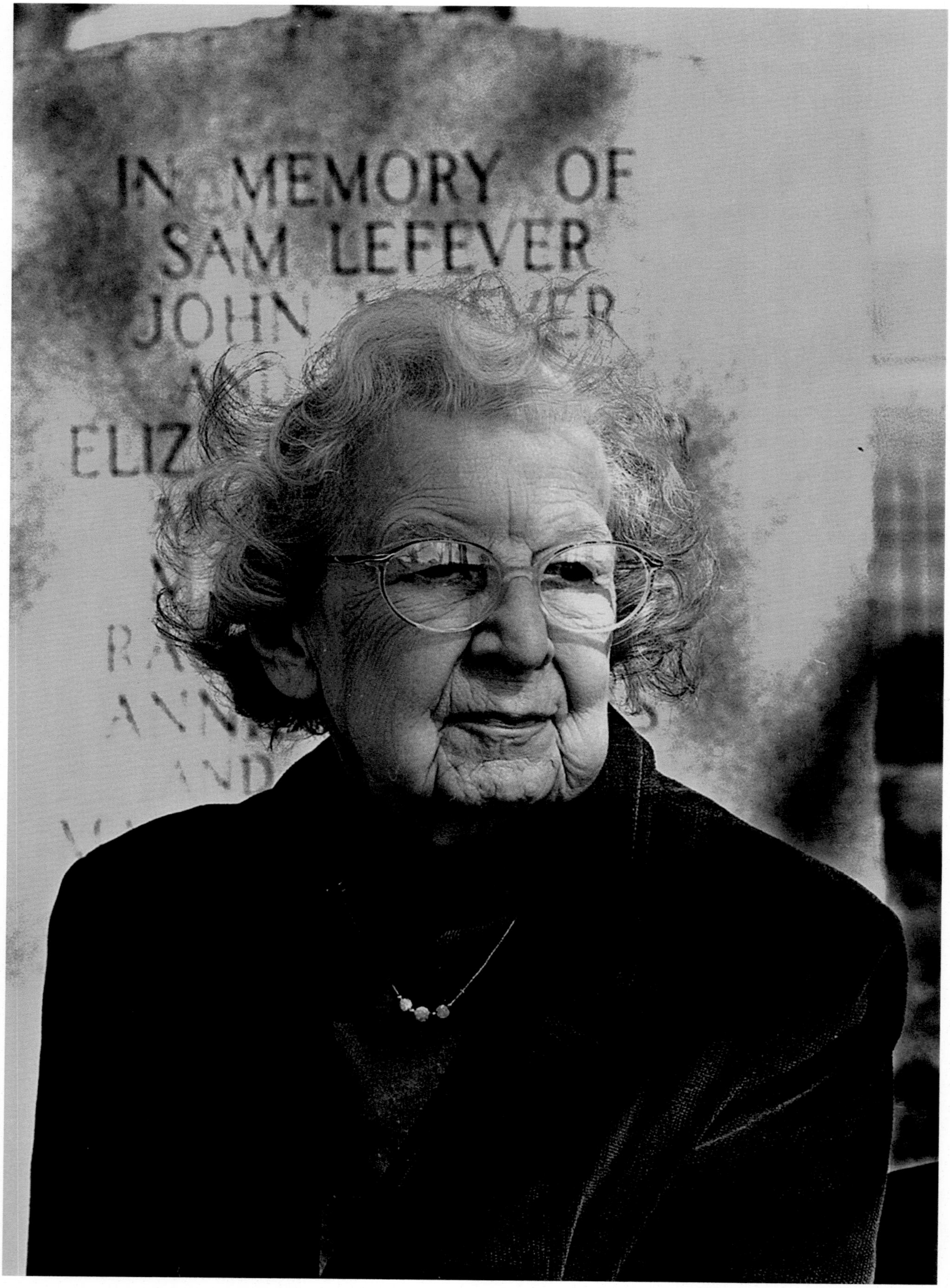
IN MEMORY OF
SAM LEFEVER
JOHN

I grew up in Ryan, which was two miles down the road from Ashburn. The middle of the town was where five roads came together. Now they've closed off two of those roads, and Ryan isn't there anymore. They've built up all around it.

There were a lot of dairy farms all around when I lived there, and I can remember hearing those generators start up early in the mornings, one right after the other. We didn't have electricity then, and the generators were used to cool the milk down.

I went to school in a one-room schoolhouse. It's still standing, but someone lives in it now. And I went to high school in Ashburn during the depression. There were only five of us in my graduating class, and I was Valedictorian.

My dad carried the mail from the Ashburn train station and took it to the post offices in Ryan, Waxpool, Arcola, and Lenah. That was in the '30s and '40s. The railroad came out from Washington and went as far as Bluemont. It started out as a passenger train and then, after the war, it was used for freight. That train would stop almost anywhere to pick up people along the way, and there were other places where it would stop so the farmers could put the milk on the train. That old train route was paved over—it's the W&OD Trail now.

My dad's family's house is still in Ryan, and the family graveyard is there too, right across the street from the old house. They put a nice iron fence around it, the developer did.

I don't remember when it happened. One development just led to another. I never thought it would turn out to be like this.

Betty Cook

Betty LeFevre Cook lives in Ashburn Village just down the road from the site of the old Ashburn train station. The village of Ryan, where she was born and raised, was one of the original towns of Loudoun County.

My father opened this hardware store in 1914. It was called Nichols and Warner then.

Long before I had a driver's license, I'd spend all day Saturdays hauling merchandise from the train station to the store. Almost all of our merchandise came by rail. We'd unload it from the boxcars and store it in the west end of the building. Half of that building was warehouse, and the other half was the train station's office and two waiting rooms—one for white people and one for blacks—and the station master had an office with a service window to each.

We sold a tremendous amount of fence and barbed wire, and I'll tell you, you don't have any trouble sleeping at night after you unload a carload of that. We sold harnesses and horse collars and pads, and now we don't carry any of those things. And we sold a lot of horseshoes. Another thing we used to sell a tremendous number of—in fact, we'd get tractor trailer loads of them—was lard cans. Not many people today know what a lard can is, I bet. It's what you put the lard in from a butchering, and, if you get a big fat hog, you've got a lot of lard. The cans come in two sizes—50 and 25 pounds. Now they're used for anything but.

How do we find things in all those drawers back here? Well, I guess you have to grow up with it. Trouble is now there are more sizes, more colors, or a whole new line of something, so we move this over here and there and it changes things. Makes it harder to remember where things are.

Ed Nichols

The Nichols family is one of the founding families of Loudoun. Born and raised in Purcellville, Ed Nichols and his brothers gradually took over the family business that their father began in 1914. Today, Nichols Hardware is a Purcellville landmark, supplying everything from housewares to building and garden materials, including lard cans.

In my day the sheriff bought everything, and we weren't paid so good either. But we bought everything we needed out of that pay. Boots, belt, even my own car. That's the truth. I had a Ford and I painted it white and put the sheriff's name on it.

My wife cooked for the prisoners in those days, too. Yep. Three meals a day.

We had an old man, Sloan, who was the town drunk, and I had to take him in every now and then. He was pretty harmless, so most of the time I'd just send for his son to take him home. Well, one night when Sloan had too much to drink, I couldn't find the boy, so I drove the old man home myself. Sloan's house set about a half a mile off the road, and the road to it was real muddy and rutted all to hell, so I figured it wouldn't be such a good idea to drive the rest of the way.

But I wanted to get him to the house as quick as I could. So, I stopped the car and turned to him, and I said, "Sloan, I'm going to run you a foot race to the house, and if you get there first, just go right on inside and sleep it off. If I get there first I'm going to take you back to jail."

Well, I had no intention of racing him to the house, of course. That old Sloan—he took off like a rabbit, but he didn't get very far. I can still hear him hollering in the dark, "T'aint fair, t'aint fair, I slipped in a rut!"

Roger Powell

A lifelong resident of Loudoun, Roger Powell spent his career in law enforcement. He served as Sheriff of Loudoun County from 1952 to 1959 and was also a member of the Leesburg Police force. After he retired, he moved to Lovettsville. He was 93 years old when he died in 2001.

My daddy was one of the leading breeders of thoroughbreds in Virginia, and he knew a lot about horses. He taught us how to ride and how to care for them, and he taught us about responsibility and respect.

We always broke our own ponies when we were growing up. They're all basically the same, but some of them give you a harder time than others. Sometimes the hardest horses to break end up being the best ones, like people.

Daddy taught me what to look for in a young horse, and I have a pretty good eye for it. I feel out their temperaments and see if they act nervous or flighty. I also try to find out about the mare's background, because that passes on. But sometimes you just have to take a chance, and I've made a few mistakes.

I've been riding horses since I was about three. People didn't give riding lessons then; we just got out there and rode and kept working at it. Later on, when I taught my children to ride, my neighbors started begging me to teach their kids. That's how it all started forty years ago, and I've been teaching kids ever since. Now I'm teaching their children's kids. My grandchildren too, they've been riding since they were three.

I can teach almost anyone to ride a horse, but it depends on how much desire they have. A lot of people get on a horse and think they can just do it, but they have to want to work at it to get it right. I make the kids learn how to do everything, because the more they get to know the horses and be around them, the better riders they become.

I've been around horses all my life, and I'm still learning.

Nancy Dillon

Nancy Dillon grew up on the Graham Horse Farm outside of Purcellville. She has been operating her own farm in Philomont for over 40 years with her husband. Also a riding instructor, Nancy teaches students of all ages and abilities to ride and to care for horses.

I was born in the brick house on the corner of Loudoun and King Streets. When I lived there, there were eight grocery stores right up the block. Now I don't expect you can buy a loaf of bread in downtown Leesburg.

After the war, I worked at the People's National Bank, which is where the Lightfoot Restaurant is now. The People's Bank was formed in the 1880s by my grandfather, his brother-in-law, who was Judge McCabe, and Colonel White. The Loudoun Bank was right across the street. It was the oldest and it was there first, but it catered to people who had a lot of money. And so the People's Bank was established to take care of the local man.

I was a teller. I worked there for 26 years, and I had a lot of customers who would come to my window. They came from all over the county, from Lucketts and even Upperville. On Saturday morning, you'd like to lock the doors to keep them out—they'd be lined up at our windows. People would come to town on Saturday to do their shopping, and visit, and take care of business. They'd be everywhere on the streets. Saturday was a big day in Leesburg then.

At one time the People's Bank had a branch in Upperville and the manager there stole money to bet on the horses. At least that's the story I heard. They closed that branch over there and brought the tellers over to work in Leesburg.

We never had much trouble at our bank. One of the fellows—the son of the bank president, McIntosh, he was the head teller—put $500 of nickels in a bag to send to the Treasury. We were only allowed to send $200 in a bag, so our bank lost $300. But that was the only trouble we ever had.

Emory Plaster

Born in 1916, Emory Plaster worked at the People's Bank from 1946 to 1970 and then became Treasurer for the Town of Leesburg. His grandfather built the current county courthouse, and his great grandfather owned Norris Mill. Emory was active with many local organizations including the Loudoun Historical Society, the Loudoun Museum, and the Town of Leesburg's Board of Architectural Review. He died in 2002.

I grew up in Philomont, but I couldn't go to the school there because I was black. So I walked to a school in St. Louis all of my elementary years. That was five-and-a-half miles each way. The school buses would pass us in the morning hauling the white kids, and the kids on the bus would be hollering and yelling at us and poking their tongues out and all. We just kept walking. Anything else and we would have ended up in a world of trouble.

The schoolhouse was over there where the Department of Transportation is now, and at one time our teacher had 76 kids in one room. And she was in charge! If she had had horns, I don't think the kids would have been any more scared of her.

She'd let us out of school early and, when we got home, we'd have work to do. We had just over seven acres, and we had cows and chickens, water to carry, wood to cut, a huge garden to work in, and hogs to feed. We used to shell corn and grind it in the coffee grinder and mama would make corn meal.

Sometimes we'd kill a chicken for dinner, but mostly we had a lot of meatless meals— big pots of dried beans and cornbread, and that was it. We didn't have to buy much; we grew almost everything we ate. Believe it or not, we'd have dessert maybe twice a week— apple cobbler, apple dumplings—sometimes mama would make a cake.

There was no place for us to go to high school. If it hadn't been for going into the army, I'd have ended up with an elementary school education.

Asbury Lloyd

Asbury Lloyd grew up with five brothers and four sisters in Philomont. He has worked all over the county, including caretaking Shelburne Glebe Plantation outside of Leesburg. Today he lives in Lincoln and is the Chairman of the Deacon Board at Mount Olive Baptist Church. Two of his sisters live in the family's homeplace in Philomont.

I was born and raised in Middleburg. Back then the town was made up of houses, not the businesses that line the streets today. We had everything we needed—in fact, we had more then than we have now in some respects. Today, I can't even find a mechanic in town to fix my car.

It was the late '20s when wealthy foxhunters from upstate New York and the Midwest really began buying and building up the surrounding countryside. Later, in the '30s, the celebrities started coming to live in the area. They could come and enjoy themselves without worrying about being bothered by anyone. A number of celebrities have lived or visited here: John Warner, Errol Flynn, Bing Crosby, Prince Ali Khan, the Smothers Brothers, Elizabeth Taylor, Jack Kent Cook, the Kennedys, the Mellons, the Whitneys, and others.

But the locals never made living here uncomfortable for them. It was the out-of-towners who were the nosey ones. There were always gawkers coming to town wanting to find someone or other. In the '60s, they'd come from all over looking for President John F. Kennedy's house. His wife, you know, was an accomplished horsewoman who rode with the local hunts.

Well, we'd see those out-of-state license plates coming, and the people would lean out their car windows and ask us, "Hey, bub, where does the president live?" We'd give them lengthy directions, and I think they'd end up somewhere around Purcellville.

Nancy Gartrell Lee

A life-long resident of Middleburg, Nancy Lee worked for the Middleburg Chronicle (now Chronicle of the Horse) for 13 years. She went on to write about thoroughbred breeding farms in Virginia, and her columns appeared in the Daily Racing Form and the Old Morning Telegraph. In 1961 she began Lee Advertising Agency out of the basement of her home in Middleburg. Today she runs the business from her office in town.

I've moved four times and haven't been off this farm. Not many people have done that. I was born right here—my sister and brothers were too. We're sixth generation.

I've farmed this land ever since I could walk. We had 132 acres and an 18-acre wood lot, and we had hired help. They didn't know the first thing about farming, and we had to show them how to do just about everything. Most of them turned out to be pretty good workers.

We ran cattle and we had sheep and hogs, and we had crops in hay, alfalfa, corn, and orchard grass. The Farmer's Almanac was our bible. We planted by the signs and wouldn't sow a seed until the sign was right. When I was growing up, we farmed the land with horses. We thrashed wheat, and we had four teams of horses that we swapped out day after day. When we worked the horses like that we'd be sure to stop every once in a while and walk around each horse to make sure it was breathing right.

It was a family operation. We didn't buy anything at the store except sugar and seasonings. We made our own flour and cornmeal. We'd take so many bushels of wheat to the mill down the road, and we'd get so many pounds of flour back; the same with corn. When that mill burned down, we'd go to Leesburg and, later, to Berryville. We quit milling our crops in 1945.

I don't believe there's a farmer living who would sell his farm if he was making a halfway decent living. And I never thought it would happen to me. But five years ago I put about 120 acres of the farm into housing lots. It's the only way I could get my retirement.

Francis Peacock

Now retired on his family farm in Paeonian Springs, Francis Peacock farmed his land until 1997. The Peacock family has been in Loudoun since the 1800s, and the sixth and seventh generations reside on six of the original acres.

I always liked this store, so when it came up for sale I thought maybe I should try it. I came over here one day and asked Alec Walsh, "How'd you like to sell the store?" and he said he'd give me the damn thing.

In the '70s and '80s, we were really busy. People coming in here all the time. We sold shoes, jeans, hardware, clothes, groceries—and we sold a lot. We sold flour in the 25-pound bags, and we had good customers.

Then the hardware man went out of business, and the small companies we dealt with started selling out to bigger companies, and the bigger companies want you to buy a certain amount of stuff or they won't deliver. So you've got to drive somewhere and get it yourself. It's been a problem for the last two years or so.

I lost the gas business in 1998. The EPA said the tanks didn't meet the new standards and they had to come out. They wanted $23,000 to install a new tank and I said, "Forget it!" Now people have to drive into town to get a gallon of gas for their lawnmower, and while they're there, they buy their milk and bread too.

The business has changed a lot. Used to be farmers coming in here. Most of my business now is construction workers. Back in 1988, we could hardly handle things here at lunchtime there were so many people coming in. Then it started dropping down and then picked up again here lately, and now it's dropping off again. The economy has slowed up.

If I keep this store until the end of the year, it'll be a miracle.

Stanley Lickey

Born and raised in Loudoun, Stanley Lickey has owned and operated the Philomont Store since 1979. He has been chief of the Philomont Fire Department since 1972 and is responsible for all its operations. He farms land near Philomont. Reproduction courtesy of Loudoun Magazine, Amendment I Inc.

I built my little house on a Wednesday. I was working at the hospital then, and I could afford $8,ooo and that was absolutely it. Mr. Arl Curry said he could build me my house, and if I let him have the job right away he would do it for that price and get me under cover before the snow came.

I wanted to talk to Mr. Curry about a few more things, but my step-son Winslow said to me, "Listen, you are not even to talk to Curry or you'll end up breaking your contract." Curry evidently wasn't used to doing business with women. So, Curry stood here and I stood there with Winslow, and I said, "Mr. Curry, I want a long, low house." Well, he just looked at me, and so Winslow said, "Arl, she wants a long, low house." And Curry replied to him, "And she shall have it." And Winslow turned to me and said, "That's all right."

And I continued, "Listen, I don't want little narrow, pig-eyed windows, I want an extra pane and width." Winslow repeated this to Curry, and Curry said, "She shall have it." And so we carried on this fantastic conversation among the three of us.

And Mr. Curry built me my house. He poured a cement base in the morning, and that night when I returned from the hospital there were cars and trucks lined up here with headlights on the house as the workers hammered the tiles on the roof. They simply worked on it all day and night!

JoanWilliams

Joan Williams lives in Leesburg in the long, low house built by Mr. Arl Curry.
Retired now after many years of dedicated service to Loudoun Hospital,
Mrs. Williams gives lively tours of Oatlands Plantation.
Reproduction courtesy of Loudoun Art, Amendment I Inc.

My first job was right here in this neighborhood with Bessie and Lula Davis. They were missionaries, and they were always giving work to the kids around town. They had 5-cent kids, 10-cent kids, and 25-cent kids. When you first started working for them, you were a 5-cent kid. That was pulling weeds in the flower garden, cutting grass, and picking up sticks. You had to work your way up. 25-cent kids got to work inside the house. Sometimes there'd be eight to ten kids working over there, and they'd make us lunch and lemonade.

We never had any trouble finding work. There was a farmer named Hume, and he'd buy Texas cattle and have them shipped to Leesburg. They'd unload the cattle right over there by South Street, and a bunch of us kids would drive the cattle all the way through town to his farm on Dry Mill Road. Mr. Hume would be in front walking and hollering, and the cattle would follow him, and we'd walk alongside of them.

I don't know if you know this or not, but people used to burn corncobs to start fires in their wood stoves. We'd go down to the mills early in the morning, and we'd take our burlap bags and our wagons and carts, load up with corn cobs, and take off through the town. Sold them for 5 cents a bag.

You know where Tuscarora Creek is? We called that the Town Branch, and we swam in it when we were young. One weekend we dammed up the creek to make our own swimming pool. Well, the Leesburg Laundry used to get their water from that creek to wash their clothes with, and when they came to work Monday morning, there was just a trickle of water coming through. They walked up the creek and saw what happened. The laundry had to wait a few days before they could wash clothes again.

Pete Roberts

Born in Leesburg as Edward Taylor Roberts, Pete has lived in town most of his life. He spent many years working with horses, both on the track and in Taylorstown in the training barn at the Firestone Farm. Now formally retired, he continues to work for several Leesburg businesses.

I grew up on our family farm when Hamilton was the second largest town in the county. There were a lot of shops there then, and people would come from all around to market. We had two newspapers. We even had a baseball team.

But aside from baseball, there wasn't a lot to do around here except talk. And the church didn't allow much else. For me, foxhunting was really the only game in town.

The records of the Loudoun Hunt go back as far as 1890. I guess when it started it was mostly the men who rode with the hunt, but the ladies soon joined in. Foxhunting was the sport that brought the local people together.

Judge Alexander was the Master of the Loudoun Hunt when I was young, and I would follow along the hillside to watch. Sometimes the hunt would meet in Leesburg and ride as far as Fairfax County. When I got a bit older, I had a terrific hound, and I would hunt on my own or I'd go with the group. Either way, it was always a challenge.

And it was serious business too. We'd gather here or at another meeting place, and if the hounds picked up a scent, off we'd go. I think the longest run I ever had from here was to Middleburg, to the East end of town. The fox we were chasing made his way over to Aldie and then to Mountville. Clayton Kephart and I pretty much stayed together and the rest of the foxhunters were all strung out behind us. It can get really chaotic with a lot of hounds.

Of course, the land has changed hands, and there are fewer places to ride now, but the hunt is still active in the county. Those foxes are still bringing people together.

Dr. Joe Rogers

An avid foxhunter for over 60 years, Dr. Joe Rogers also practiced medicine for 30 years in Leesburg. But his first love has always been farming. He and his family have farmed their land in and around Hamilton since 1794, for over five generations.

When we came to live in Loudoun, we weren't hampered by planning and zoning issues. We decided where we wanted to buy land and we bought it. We decided where we wanted to put our house and we put it there. There were no regulations on what we did.

I persuaded the Board of Supervisors to appoint a planning commission to investigate whether zoning would be beneficial to the county. The Supervisors voted in favor of it, but they didn't set up any staff and they didn't provide any money. They didn't do anything! Carol Cornwell—she was right out of school then—and I ran the Planning Commission from my house for the first year of its existence.

We didn't have anything, but we just did it. When people finally began asking for permits to build, the County hadn't provided any forms, and so Carol and I would create them. I'd get a call from someone in the county building telling me there was somebody there who wanted a permit to build a house, and I'd say, "Tell him to wait" and I'd get in the car and go chasing into Leesburg. After some time the supervisors saw that it wasn't the best way to run a government, and so they gave us an office— a tiny room with a desk and a table. I remember the desk very well because the drawer contained Sheriff's summons and they read, "Failure to respond to this summons to be subject to a fine of not more than 100 pounds sterling." That's how up-to-date we were.

After about a year, Carol was made Zoning Administrator. Now I look at the staff—I think there are 70 people there now, and room after room—and I think, whatever did we start?

Vinton Pickens

Vinton Pickens came to Loudoun County in 1934. A political activist, she was the driving force behind the anti-billboard ordinance, one of the first in the US. She served on the County's planning commission for 21 years, from 1940–1961. Vinton was also a painter and founded the Loudoun Sketch Club in 1944. She died in 1993.
Story courtesy of Thomas Balch Library

Eugene: Sure, I remember prohibition. And I remember when the feds came out here one time. Mr. Lindsay was the deputy sheriff, and he came over to my dad's sawmill. Said he was going to raid the still across the way and wanted to know how to get to the place. Well, I was working at the sawmill, and I could hear what they were talking about. Course, I'd bought moonshine off the guy. So while they were talking to my dad, I swung across the road and went and told him to git and hide because the revenue men were coming. They didn't catch him, but they cut his still all up. Dad got on me for telling him to run. I never knew that feller's name—I never asked him any questions.

Renace: That old sawmill was on down the Holler Road and up over the hill. We named it the Old Holler Road, and that's what everybody back here calls it. We used to get old snuff boxes and tie them together with a string and we'd holler back and forth on it, like a telephone.

The Stoney Road down the way was built by taking all of the rocks out of the road and making stone fences. The WPA built that road and also built the waterline that connected the three springs together. The first pipe had started to deteriorate—it was old wooden pipe with creosote on it wrapped with wire. So they took out the wooden pipe and replaced it with cast iron. That was in the '30s during the Depression. The WPA built the entire waterline by hand—every bit of it—and it goes down to the river, crosses the riverbed and goes over to Brunswick.

(continued)

Eugene and Renace Painter

Eugene and Renace Painter are two of the nine Painter children who grew up in Painter's Corner at the far end of Lovettsville. Eugene worked on the railroad from 1936 to 1980, starting as a carpenter and retiring as a mechanic. Today, he lives in Frederick, Maryland. Renace Painter still lives in Lovettsville, just a few miles from the old Painter homestead. Retired from the government, he uses his handyman skills to help his neighbors and friends. Painters Corner was named after Eugene and Renace's father who ran a sawmill business and later worked on the railroad.

Eugene: The WPA brought loads of people over here to work on that waterline—30 or 40 men at a time, maybe. The WPA camp was in Round Hill, I think, and they brought men over by the truckload. It took them three years to do the work. Well, they didn't work that hard.

Renace: They took the stone fence that went from the corner and used the rocks to build up a piece of the road. They'd bust up the rocks to make them smaller, and one of those guys busted one open and found a piece of gold in it. Remember that, Eugene? Well, that was it! Everybody was up there; they were busting up every rock they could find. Now, Eugene here tells me that the gold is hid up here next to the Cool Spring. When they ran the Indians out of this area, they buried their gold up there somewhere. If you go to the Cool Spring, you can see the old Indian burial ground.

Eugene: I can take you up there and show you the arrows they've got on the rocks, but I never could find the gold. They tell me the Indians brought it in here in buffalo hides and buried it. I think it's up there on the mountain.

Renace: Yes, ma'am. There's a lot of good memories up in this corner.

Many people have supported and encouraged us as we worked on this project. We are most grateful to our friends Frannie Taylor, Joan Williams, Arlene Janney, Jill Beach, Sheila Kryston, Carolyn Unger, and Peggy King, whose support made this book possible.

Special thanks are due to Henry Taylor, poet and Pulitzer Prize winner, for writing the Foreword, Dr. Dave Williams for his mastery of punctuation and the serial comma, Bill Marable for several story origins, Janet Matthews for supplying the photograph of her grandmother, the late Vinton Pickens, and Mouncey Ferguson for taking the group photo on the back cover.

The Thomas Balch Library in Leesburg was a source of many of the reference materials used to supplement and verify the stories on these pages, and the Loudoun Historical Society was a source of encouragement and support. More enthusiasm came from Meredith Bean McMath, Peter Burnett, and Tom Jewell.

Personal thanks go to Lisa Hawthorne for creating the book's design, and Claire Coughter, whose knowledge of paper and print helped produce the book. Above all, we want to thank the people whom we celebrate in this book for the gifts they share with all of us.

Acknowledgments

Sarah Huntington has been photographing Loudoun's personalities since 1980, shortly after she moved to Virginia. A graduate of the Corcoran School of Art, Sarah owns and operates her studio in Purcellville, Virginia where she makes her living photographing people and events. A native of Greenville, South Carolina, she combines her southern roots with her sense of history and art to create revealing images.

Gale Waldron has lived in Loudoun since 1985. A writer, editor and fine art consultant, she became interested in the area's history when she met Asa Moore Janney at the Lincoln store. Gale began interviewing and writing about some of Loudoun's characters for a local newspaper and, in 1998, she founded Loudoun ART magazine. She now writes about people and the arts for several local and regional publications.

Both women live in and around Lincoln, where they appreciate small town living. This book is a blend of their talents and friendship.

Printed in the United States
By Bookmasters